Bread Comes to Life

A Garden of Wheat and a Loaf to Eat

by George Levenson
Photography by Shmuel Thaler

Tricycle Press
Berkeley | Toronto

Bread is the food we eat every day.

So many kinds. So many ways.

White bread.

Black bread.

Small bread.

Tall bread.

Thin bread.

Twin bread.

Dinner rolls.

Bread with holes.

Hard, day-old tough bread.

Soft, squishy fluff bread.

Bread is toast.

Bread is crumbs.

Bread is pizza.

Bread is buns.

How is bread made?

Where is it from?

This baker

makes his bread

from scratch

by sowing wheat

in his backyard patch.

Soon those seeds send down roots

and sprout into shoots of bright green grass.

The days pass

and that grass

grows into

sturdy blades,

tall and straight,

finely made

with budding heads

and bristly hair

gently waving in the air.

When the crop is

ripe and old,

the tops are bowed

and streaked with gold.

And every head of

wheat contains

many tiny finished grains.

Time to cut the golden field.

Gather up the backyard yield.

Stack up piles of sun-dried stalks.

Rub them in a threshing box.

It's the simple, old-time miller's craft

of separating wheat from chaff.

What's left

are seeds,

a hefty load,

many times

the number

sowed.

And each new grain of harvest wheat

looks just like a loaf to eat.

Now is the hour

to grind those grains

into whole wheat flour.

With simple tools and easy rules,

it's on with the show to make up some dough

and bring fresh bread to life.

Yeast. Honey. Water. Flour.

Salt.

Oil.

And muscle power.

Dump it.

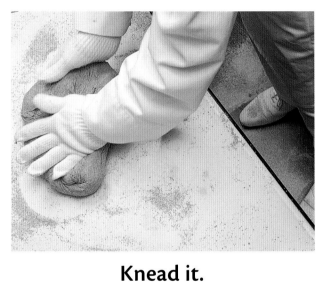

Thump it.

Dust it.

Knead it.

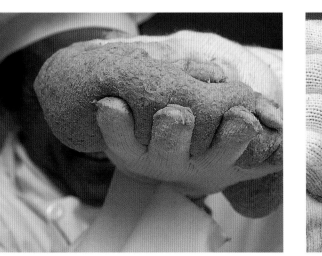

Squash it.

Stretch it.

Set it aside to rest and rise.

It grows and grows to twice the size.

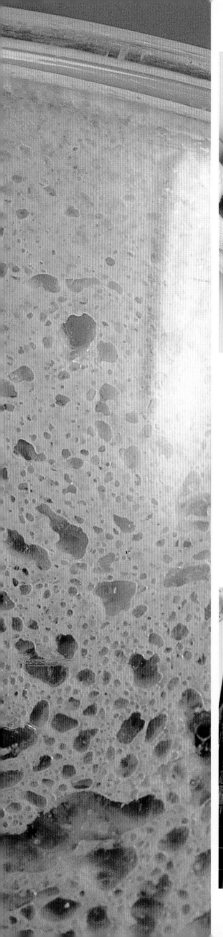

Punch it down.

Give it some shape.

Let it rise again.

Put it in to bake.

Slice it fresh.

It's better than cake!

Whatever the shape it finally takes,

wherever the place it finally bakes,

every day we are blessed

with a mountain of bread.

It's the staff of life.

May all be fed.

Wheat is Neat

Wheat is planted all over the world in every season. It doesn't need much water, and its roots can reach thirty feet into the earth. There are over 150 common varieties, some

of which grow seven feet tall! One grain of wheat can produce eight or more heads with over forty seeds per head. And the grains harvested from one acre—about the size of a football field—can provide a family of four with enough flour to make bread for ten years.

Wheat is Grain—Grow a Plot

You don't have to live on a farm to plant a crop of wheat. Look for whole grains in natural foods stores and on the Internet. Hard red winter wheat, the best type for bread, is usually planted in November, before the first frost. For a backyard crop, sow the seeds 1 inch deep and 1 inch apart in rows, allowing 6 inches between rows. The seeds will mature in about 8 months.

Wheat is Grass— Sprout a Pot

Plant a plot in a pot and watch the seeds grow into lush grass.

1. Fill a 4 ounce container with potting soil.
2. Spread seeds on the surface of the soil. Do not overlap them.

3. Cover seeds with a thin layer of soil, like a blanket.
4. Water daily. Keep the soil moist but not drenched.

In 5 to 7 days, the seeds will sprout into bright green blades. When they are about 6 inches tall, pinch off 10 blades and chew them up. The sweet, strong-tasting juice, rich in chlorophyll, is said to hold 92 of the 102 minerals found in soil, as well as almost all the vitamins humans need. Cats like the grass, too.

Wheat is Gum—Double your Fun

Before there was chewing gum in the store, farmers made their own with grains of wheat. So can you!

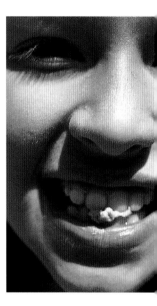

Place 50 grains of hard red winter wheat in your mouth, crunch down slowly, and start chewing. Your jaw and teeth become a stone grinder, and you will immediately taste the nutty flavor of whole wheat. Chew for a few minutes, making sure to swallow the excess saliva but not the grains. Soon you will have a little mound of dough in your mouth. Keep chewing, and it will become a smooth, long-lasting lump of pure wheat gluten, or old-fashioned farmer's gum.

What about that Rootin' Tootin' Gluten?

Gluten, a stretchy, sticky protein found in wheat, helps bread to rise. Here's how it works: When baker's yeast is mixed with flour and water and kneaded into a dough, the yeast cells divide and give off tiny bubbles of carbon dioxide. The gluten in the dough traps these bubbles, forming little balloons that expand and make the dough rise. You can see a cross section of the bubbles in every slice of bread.

Wheat is Bread— Bake a Loaf

Bread is probably the most ancient food that is still part of the modern diet. The very first bread was a loose mixture of crushed whole grains and water blended into gruel and then flattened to dry in the sun or bake over an open fire. Today, most people believe they don't have the time or know-how to make their own bread, yet the tools and ingredients are readily available. Here's a recipe for a 100% whole wheat loaf that any 4-year-old, with an adult helper, can make.

> $1^1/_2$ cups lukewarm water, $^1/_4$ cup honey, 1 packet active dry yeast, $^1/_4$ cup vegetable oil, 2 teaspoons salt, and $3^1/_2$ cups whole wheat bread flour

Mixing: Set aside $^1/_2$ cup of the flour. Combine the rest of the ingredients in a large bowl, stirring them together in the order listed. Stir until it begins to form a lump. Lightly dust the table top with some of the reserved flour and turn the dough out onto it. Let it rest for 10 minutes.

Kneading: Dust your hands with flour and begin kneading. First, gently push the dough away from you so that it flattens out, then give it a quarter turn, and fold it in half toward you. Push, turn, and fold. Repeat the process about 100 times, dusting your hands and the table with flour, a sprinkle at a time, to prevent sticking. The dough is ready when it is as soft and tender as your earlobe. Shape the dough into a ball.

Rising: Roll the dough inside an oiled bowl so that it is evenly coated. Cover with a dishcloth or plastic wrap, and let the dough rise at room temperature until doubled in size, about 1 hour. Punch down the dough to release the carbon dioxide, then turn the dough out onto the table top. Knead it another 50 times to develop the gluten further and to squeeze out the carbon dioxide.

Shape the dough into a rectangle, and press it into a greased bread pan ($8^1/_2$-by-$4^1/_2$ inches). Cover with a cloth, and let the dough rise half an inch above the rim.

Baking: Bake at 350° for 30 to 45 minutes. Remove the loaf from the pan and tap the bottom of the loaf. A clear, hollow sound means it's done.

When you have gained confidence, double the recipe. Giving a loaf to a friend is a precious gift of caring and love.

For more details about wheat and bread, watch the companion video and visit *www.breadcomestolife.com*.

Tricycle Press
an imprint of Ten Speed Press
PO Box 7123
Berkeley, California 94707
www.tricyclepress.com

Cover design by Jean Sanchirico
Interior design by Tasha Hall
Typeset in Cronos

Library of Congress Cataloging-in-Publication Data

Levenson, George.
    Bread comes to life : a garden of wheat and a loaf to eat / by George
Levenson; photography by Shmuel Thaler.
        p. cm.
    1. Bread—Juvenile literature. 2. Wheat—Juvenile literature. I. Title.
    TX769.L43 2004
    641.8'15—dc22
                                                                2004002551

First Tricycle Press printing, 2004
First paperback printing, 2008
Printed in China

ISBN: 978-1-58246-114-4 hc/ 2 3 4 5 6 7 — 10 09 08 07 06
ISBN: 978-1-58246-273-8 pbk/ 1 2 3 4 5 6 — 12 11 10 09 08